NER
Crushing It!

Michelle Kaplan

and

A love story within

MICHELLE J. KAPLAN

Praise for *and: A love story within*

Michelle Kaplan's keen awareness of the truth of our human experience and her transparent vulnerability combined with her personal quest for freedom and self-expression make reading her poetry a deep and meaningful experience.

~ **Jack Canfield, Coauthor of the *Chicken Soup for the Soul* series and *The Success Principles™: How to Get from Where You Are to Where You Want to Be***

Michelle Kaplan set out on a journey to find herself amid all the inner and outer confusions and complexities of life. Many readers will find their own story in hers, and will find her poetry inspiring and empowering as they set out to do what she did: reconnect with themselves, and live out the love affair between 'soul and ego, heart and mind, love and fear, heaven and earth.' There's a love story within all of us waiting to be written and rewritten, the kind of self-love without which all other love fails. May this book help you find, write, and live your inner love story.

~ **Parker J. Palmer, Author of *Let Your Life Speak, A Hidden Wholeness, and On the Brink of Everything***

Michelle Kaplan's poems have a way of latching onto ones' soul and provides a sense of inner peace and freedom.

~ **Jean Marie Rosone, LCSW, Coordinator of Integrative Oncology, Carol G. Simon Cancer Center, Morristown Medical Center**

It took reading *and: a love story within* for me to realize that my conscious mind assumed "and" was a decision to be made, a conscious choice about how to live. No. It's present in everyday living, striving and inclusive, a gift that is given, if only we can see. This book puts words to the inner knowings we all have, yet so easily dismiss. "And" gives permission to listen to the clear, steady, and persistent inner voice and in doing so fully become ourselves.

~ **Michelle Arpin Begina, Senior Partner/Managing Director Wealth Advisory Firm**

and: a love story within is a mirror of your most inner thoughts and struggles. Self-reflections are brought to the surface that have been buried over time. It tugs at your soul and reminds you of who you once were and who you can rediscover.

~ **Rosemarie M.**

This book will touch your heart! As you read it, over and over again, you will be inspired and you will belly laugh! Like a dear friend you really trust, it will speak to you in the challenging moments of life. And—it will support you on your journey of True Self discovery and transformation!

~ **Mitch Rosacker, Self Discovery Studio**

"Though a personal journey of her own awareness, Michelle Kaplan's poems enabled me to place myself in the story as if it was written for me. It put words to my own personal experiences that I had not found for myself. Thank you for sharing your journey, the good, the bad, and the ugly. What is wonderful is that it shows that the journey to self-awareness unfolds in many stages, but in the end, the power of knowing who you are allows you to live life with one of the most wonderful people on this earth...yourself."

~ **Cindy Tomcak, Performance Coach**

Michelle Kaplan allowed me to know her inner feelings and truths through her beautiful, inspiring and honest poetry. As she delves into her realities, fears and discoveries, she has encouraged me to do the same. I too, have searched all my life for the answers and through her insightful writing and creativity in *and: A love story within*, I was provided a guide to find my own inner voice and self.

~ **Diana B.**

Through her magical words and open heart, Michelle Kaplan awakens all our senses with her raw honesty, authenticity, and emotional journey of self-discovery. Although a deeply personal story woven together poem by poem, *and: A love story within* is amazingly relatable and universal, automatically inviting the reader to contemplate their own soul's adventure. As you get to know the author, you cannot help but more precisely know yourself, a true sign of a masterpiece.

~ **Cindy D. Whitmer, Coach, Speaker, Author, Founder of The Inspiration Center**

Your words are like fingers touching my body, arousing me so.

~ **Jillian Marty Dushane, Ph.D. Candidate, Communication, UMass Amherst**

and: A love story within

MICHELLE J. KAPLAN

Table of Contents

The Invitation to *and*

Come dream with me.

The night is still young.

We can go wherever we desire,

do the unthinkable,

and create the unimaginable.

Anything is possible

with a moon so full and bright.

So take my hand.

It's time to go.

Come dream with me.

Foreword

I first met Michelle at one of Jack Canfield's Train the Trainer programs after my stage demonstration of the RIM® Method, a body-centered transformational technique that I discovered. Her vitality and exuberance for life was immediately apparent and now I know why. She has what many people don't—an intimate connection with herself.

The writing of poetry has provided Michelle a safe place to explore her demons. Little did she know how much richer and more expressive her life could be. In essence when she wrote the poetry book *and*, she reconnected with her soul. She fell in love with herself.

Since our first meeting, Michelle has trained with me and is a Certified RIM® Facilitator. Many times, we've shared our love of how images shape and transform our lives—whether through an imaginary adventure with The RIM® Method or through the writing or reading of poetry. Both experiences can take us to unknown destinations beyond the logical mind, yet offer answers to what really matters most—the true self.

Poetry has transformed my life also. In my book, *Releasing the Inner Magician*, I share how spontaneous writing in a poetry class brought me release and insight that healed my relationship with my daughter.

Michelle's poetry holds great healing—healing from her own experiences—beautiful healing that readers get to share on their journey through *and*.

Deborah Sandella, PhD, RN
Founder of The RIM® Institute
Author of #1 International Bestseller, *Goodbye, Hurt & Pain: 7 Simple Steps for Health, Love, and Success*

Preface

It was more like the last straw than a big epiphany. I was just tired of feeling like it was never enough. For others. For me. I kept saying to myself, "I want to find the Truth." I didn't know exactly what that was other than to describe it as a more authentic way of being. I had this gnawing sense that there was more to life. There just had to be, because if this was it, I'm screwed.

So I started self-inquiry practices. One of them was writing to help clarify my thoughts and feelings. Through writing my musings, confessions, and insights, I had this one "aha" realization that changed everything for me. I finally understood this one simple and real truth.

I will never be enough and that I am enough.

These two simultaneous realities, paradoxical and true, made me feel hopeless and liberated at the same time. I recognized how much time and energy I spent trying to change others' perceptions of me when what I really needed to do was change *my* perception of me. Instead, I was resisting by defending, controlling, and avoiding because, whether conscious of it or not, I believed them. Yet, there was also a small, deep place within me that understood the misperceptions were a load of crap.

I wanted to connect more to that small deep place within. I knew that to do that meant that I had to start listening and acting on my inner knowings, which, at times, goes against the grain. Many times I heard from others, "Get with the program, Michelle." So I did. I really tried. But it really wasn't working for me—or them.

There were also times when I decided, with the best intentions, not to go along with what was expected because I saw another way, which caused emotional reactions in others that I either internalized or had me campaigning hard, trying to convince them somehow to accept, or dare I say, even like what I was doing. Yeah, I know. Good luck with that.

So slowly, I started to live my truths, baby steps more than giant leaps, because I wasn't really sure what was true anymore. Hence, my personal mantra was born, "Keep it simple. Keep it real." Truth asks for only that.

No one said simple and real is easy. And yet, over time, as the small, deep place within me grew larger and became more accessible; others' words and actions couldn't penetrate my new armor of enoughness. In my search for answers, I received more questions and ultimately found a love story. The inevitable love affair between my soul and ego, heart and mind, love and fear, heaven and earth. This love story is within all of us waiting to be written and rewritten.

and: a love story within is a self-transformational book written in poetic verse, stories within a story, textured and layered, of my personal journey in the universal search for Truth. The way to truth and love is a lifelong, moment-to-moment process built on the ever-growing foundation of trust as I continue to feel my way through the unsteadiness and inconsistency of living in the divine mystery in a world that demands human certainty. The offering of my poems is an invitation for you to rise up to your highest potential and create true love from the inside out since my truth is your truth.

One Truth. The Truth.

With love and gratitude,
Michelle
June 15, 2018

PROLOGUE

The Clock Watcher

I grab my folders, pack up my laptop, and head out of work.
I pass You in the hallway on my way out.
Not so subtly,
You glance at your watch and then back at me
with a look of disapproval.

At a meeting about a week ago,
You spoke to the group
about your disdain for the Clock Watchers,
the ones who leave exactly on time,
every day, no less.

They're lazy, uncaring and unaccountable,
always trying to get away with something.
There should be no tolerance for this.

It's 5:00 o'clock on the dot
and I'm hurrying out of work...
again.

I'm in my car now,
on the highway,
when I notice a sea of red
from the brake lights
of the cars stopped in traffic.
I slowly crawl through the congestion
with everyone else.

I'm getting nervous.
The clock on the dashboard reads 5:30
and I'm only half way home.
I need to pick up my daughter
from the after school program by six.

I watch a black Audi
weaving in and out of lanes,
desperately or valiantly
trying to get out of this mess.
Finally, a clearing on the road ahead.
GO!

I race the rest of my commute home,
round the corner into the school parking lot
a little faster than I should
and park the car.
5:58
Perfect.
Two minutes to spare.

As I sprint in my high heels
into the school cafeteria,
I see you sitting at a table,
all alone,
with your backpack and lunch bag by your side,
all ready to go.
Waiting.

You run into my arms
and give me a big hug,
"Momma, you came!"
"Of course, honey."
We gather your stuff and you ask me,
so gently,
so softly,
"Why am I always the last kid to be
picked up every night?"

I quickly shift my body and look away,
as I don't want you to see the tears forming,
evidence of my heart breaking.
I can barely get out the words,
"I'm so sorry."

You reply back,
"It's okay. I'm alright. How was *your* day?"
Always thinking of me.
How kind and thoughtful you are.

We rush off to dinner,
giggling and being silly
as we do your homework
at a booth at the diner.
Then off to an hour of tutoring
to help you with the subjects
you're struggling with.
You look tired
when I pick you up,
but you still have that bright smile
on your beautiful face.

I think about your day,
as an eight year old,
who left the house
at 7:45 this morning,
and twelve hours later, there is
no complaining,
no whining
after all your hard work.
Just sweetness.
How much I learn from watching you.

We get home,
get into our pj's
and cuddle on the couch,
watching your favorite show,
finally time to relax.
I put you to bed, and,
after talking time and the usual stalling,
you fall asleep with Bear Bear
tucked safely in your arms.

I, on the other hand,
head downstairs,
grab my paperwork and laptop bag
and head to the kitchen table,
to finish an assignment
that's due at the end of the week.
As I work by the glow of the light
coming off my monitor,
I think about Your view of me
as a Clock Watcher.

I don't get the glory of being the hero at work,
riding into the conference room after hours,
on my white horse,
ready to save the project from near disaster.
I don't get called up on stage at the banquet dinner
to receive an award for my tireless contributions.
No, I don't even get credit
for giving good face time
for working at my desk late into the evening.

Instead, Clock Watchers are quietly working
and eating lunch alone
because we know
we have to make the most of our time
at the office.
We continually make conflicting choices,
which school functions
to attend during work hours.
We juggle, scramble, and barter
on who is going to watch our child when they get sick,
have a miscellaneous day off from school,
or when we receive
the dreaded snow day robo-call at 5:00 a.m.

It's working diligently
at the kitchen table
until 11:30 at night
to make sure we get our work done,
whenever we can,
without anyone, but ourselves
knowing how much we accomplish.
Clock Watchers celebrate silent, solitary victories.

With these last thoughts,
my eyes close.
I fall asleep quickly.
Tomorrow's another busy day.

So I Write

And then I just know.
The tradeoff
between staying
or going to another place
that is really just more of the same
makes me feel flat.
And, anyway,
the person they want and expect,
well, she doesn't exist anymore.

I guess I was right,
they can't afford me,
no one can,
because what I'm seeking
comes from within.
It's my soul's turn
to be front and center
with the freedom
to live its intended journey.

There is no turning back.
I crossed a line
I didn't even know existed,
until now.
And it wasn't this dramatic event.
More like gentle nudges,
guiding me.
I'm finally getting quiet
to hear the loving whispers
from my essence.
I'm finally listening.

I feel regret
for living the life of an imposter
for all these years.
What a blessing
to be feeling such strain
over my charlatan ways.

Tolerable and satisfied
keeps me passive and complacent,
while the angst lets me advance,
to write,
because writing is about...
connecting to truth,
clarifying my truth,
creating from truth.
It's the act of writing
that makes this sorrow go away.

So I take one step at a time
to where I'm being led
because my soul gets
that if I understand all at once
where this is heading,
I could get stuck,
maybe even hide out.

Words are coming through me.
That I know for sure.
What comes from that,
I have no clue.
The not knowing
used to stop me
from moving forward.
Now I find it...
inviting, enticing, alluring.
Where is this all leading?

It's all so simple
and so hard,
to live in faith
when what I am being
called to become
appears right now as...
impractical, pointless, unfeasible.

I realize now
that the ego defines success
by the outcomes achieved.
While, victory for the soul
is the process itself.
So I surrender
to this unnamed longing,
and live in this creative tension.

And so I write.

PART I

The Ego...
and the suffering it creates

Message from the Tea Leaves

Let's just say it wasn't a great meeting.
In fact, the whole day at work pretty much sucked.
The blustery, gray afternoon now matches the mood
I suddenly find myself in.
A nice cup of tea beckons me.
Interesting, because I usually drink coffee,
but I'm already wired on life.

I grab my mug,
pour in some hot water
and head back to my desk.
Way in the back,
in the second drawer on the left
is a tea bag that's been there too long.
It'd have to do.

As my tea brews,
I notice, in my peripheral vision,
words on the white square piece of paper
at the end of the string
attached to the tea bag.

Be proud of who you are.

I take sips of my tea as I work,
allowing the liquid elixir to seep in,
while repeating the message,
each time slower and more deliberately,
Be...proud...of...who...you...are.

Am I proud of who I am?

Yeah, sure...
I want to believe I do,
yet the tear forming
tells me otherwise.

Velvet Coffin

Close your eyes,
be still,
and conjure up
your worst fears.

Now you have a sense
of the cage
you're imprisoned in.

Yes, at times
you've changed one
velvet coffin for another,
but it's all the same.

In the need
for control,
to feel safe,
we choose to create
our own version of Hell.

Quenching My Thirst

I'm so parched.
Mouth dry.
Lips chapped.
Can barely speak.

I keep drinking
what they're offering,
but it never satisfies me.
I still feel empty and depleted.
There has to be something
to make this thirst go away.

Seeping through cracks,
trickling out of crevices,
water stains on ceilings,
puddling in corners,
my house leaking.
I'm surrounded by water,
yet still insatiable.

Water follows the path
of least resistance.
What is my house trying to tell me?

Gypsy

Gypsy,
the great pretender,
noticed by others,
dressed in style,
working the room,
hiding,
right in front of you.

Gypsy,
chameleon,
bartering who she is
with what you want her to be
as long as you give her
what she wants.

Gypsy,
protector,
fierce like a tiger,
sly like a fox,
taking,
to then give away,
her intentions purer
than her persona.

Gypsy,
misunderstood,
watching, waiting
to expose your vulnerabilities
to her advantage,
tired of the struggle,
the drama,
and the double standard.

Little does she know
that what she wants most
to receive
is the one thing
she struggles to offer...
herself

The Red Sundress

I'm shoved in the back of her closet,
pressed between an evening gown
last worn to a wedding a few years ago
and a pair of too tight jeans
she's hoping to fit into again someday.

Once in a while,
she catches a glimpse of crimson
amongst the sea of somber tones
and looks at me wistfully.
Magnetized since she first saw me
hanging in the gift shop five years ago,
the attraction hasn't waned.

She gets hints of things she doesn't understand,
pieces of other realities she can't connect.
After all these years,
she keeps trying to solve the riddle
while waiting for the right occasion to put me on
because her life doesn't match my color and style.

Maybe, just maybe,
she needs to put me on
and wear me, finally, for
I'm not the destination.
I'm not the answer.
I'm the doorway,
the invitation,
the question.
Isn't everything that?

So Done!

You leave me feeling so uninspired,
but that's my fault, not yours.
I keep waiting for something or someone
to ignite me and save me from myself,
again and again.

Waiting for...
the right time,
when I can afford it,
a sign,
permission,
blah, blah, blah
and more blah.
I know it's the insidious voice of my fears.
Yet I still wait.
Lovely.

And I get the sense
that I've waited too long
to do something about it
because I allowed myself to believe
that this is what I should want
and that it's enough.
But now I'm left suppressing the urge
to scream from the top of my lungs
for anyone to hear,

PUT A FORK IN ME BECAUSE I'M SO DONE!

Done with settling, accommodating,
avoiding, negotiating,
in vain, as I seek your approval
that you bestow upon me, at your whim,
in teeny weeny portions,
just enough to sustain the illusion
that everything's okay.

But really, you just want to control me
and prove to yourself that you're right,
because whatever I do,
or don't,
it's never enough anyway.

I put so much energy
into trying to please you
that I'm losing me,
and I've worked too hard,
experienced too much,
and come too far
to stay where I'm at.

OVER IT!
I get it now.
And the clearer I get,
the stronger I feel,
the bolder I act, and
the weaker your influence over me becomes.

I'm sorry if being myself
makes you so uncomfortable
that you need to put me down
to feel better about you.
But now, I'm the one
out of my comfort zone,
because a safety net,
is still a net,
restricting freedom.
What was once acceptable
now feels intolerable,
and from where I'm standing,
it doesn't look too safe either.

So what do you do
when you come to realize
that your life,
the one you created,
doesn't embody who you really are?

Ummm...I think I'm about to find out.

PART 2

The Soul...
remembering who we really are

My Wish for You

I wish you could see yourself
as I see you,
because if you recognized in yourself
what I know to be true,
all the loveliness that you are,
and that you share with others,
could finally be felt
by you,
giving yourself the gift
of love, acceptance, and peace
you've been yearning for
your whole life,
that's not outside of you,
but within.

From the Silence

The sound of your soul
comes from the silence.
You need the quiet first,
to put aside
the noise and clutter
in your mind
to reach the voice of Truth,
because you hear more
than with your ears
and see more
than with your eyes.

The silence is
so gentle,
like a soft caress
against your cheeks,
so calm,
like a still body of water,
so expansive
like a clear, starry night sky.

The thoughts and feelings
that bubble up
from the silence
are your inner wisdom.
You get these knowings
from the stillness.

You may feel like
what you're receiving
isn't real.
Some may even say you're crazy
or at best, have an overactive imagination,
so you dismiss what you're sensing.

DON'T!

The messages from your soul
are telling you
who you truly are
and what you need to do
to experience your greatness.

They reflect **your** truth.

It's from this truth
that you start connecting
who you are
with what you do.

The specifics
look different for everybody,
so you'll recognize
your inspired actions
because they are things
that you love to do.
In fact, you are so passionate
about doing them
you don't want to stop,
because they bring you such joy!

Learn to trust **that** voice.

Get good at being still
so you can hear
the whispers
meant for you
and only you…
from the silence.

A Beautiful View

I'm standing on the ledge,
a precarious existence.
Glancing down,
at my bare feet,
I see the tips of my toes,
peeking out,
off the end of the rocky, gravel edge,
the backdrop,
a dark, bottomless abyss,
void of any fear.

I stand with purpose,
feeling the subtle wind
dancing around my face,
and rushing through my hair,
the power of my Being,
quickly pulsing through my veins,
my skin tingling
from the exuberance
of needing to stay present and aware,
so I don't fall off.

I feel the hot release of tears,
as I'm overcome by
the loveliness of it all.
How long can I stand here?
My footing becomes unstable,
at the thought of that,
my mind interfering again.

I look up and raise my arms up to the sky.
My whole body receives comfort
from the warmth of the sun,
offering forgiveness
at my digression.
It's all good, sweet and magical,
connected to something greater than me.

I stand on this ledge,
feeling limitless,
knowing what could be
and having no sense of what will come.
The ledge that I've unknowingly
been afraid of my whole life.
I finally stand,
feeling truly alive.

The Orange Candle

The flame reveals
that love provides
a ray of hope, courage, and comfort
to all who dare to love greatly.

The dripping wax
shows us
how soft and fluid love is.

The pool of warm wax
that takes shape
communicates that love is wordless.

The hardened wax
unveils how love can solidify
and transform.

The burned and hollowed out remains
reminds us that love isn't concerned
with how we look on the outside.
Love sees beauty from the inside out.

Our senses experience
the change in the candle's form,
disclosing the creative power
of how love changes us.

The candle has a higher purpose
as we all do,
and illuminates from its connection
to the One,
as everything does.

Love's energy
is the source
of light and life.

Silent Prayer

Unpretentious skies of blue and gray
rising through the mist.

A new dawn,
where all my fears fade away,
like the fog lifting before my eyes.

I greet the sun
with hope and gratitude
for the love in my life.

I rejoice in my silent prayer
to you and all,
as we begin anew,
in each moment,
each challenge,
each chore,
in each other.

True Nature

She is very mysterious,
this One,
who knows all,
but doesn't kiss and tell.

Gentle and soft-spoken,
all She requires is silence
to be heard.

Bigger than life,
and yet so careful with the details,
She shows her kindness
by offering what you need,
not necessarily what you desire.

Fiercely loyal and compassionate,
She is confidante, mother, and teacher,
the one we keep searching for,
though she's always there,
patiently waiting for us to come home.

Home is with you wherever you go.

Morning Meditation

I slowly awaken.
All is still and at peace
except the movement
from the ceiling fan
creating a rush of cool air
that continuously swirls over me,
gently caressing my warm, slumbered form.

My back arches
into a delicious stretch
as I burrow deeper
into the disheveled pile
of blankets and pillow,
the aftermath of my dreams in motion.

I deeply inhale
the smell of fresh linens
and the earthy scents of spring
that blows in
from the half-opened window
by my bed.
My eyes still closed.
My mind blank, open and available
to infinity's life flow.

The intimacy in the room is palpable,
indescribable.
I feel you most at this time each day
when the energies of others
aren't comingled with ours,
just you and me,
pure and sacred,
whole and complete,
reminding me of who I truly am
and what is real.

Though we are together,
always,
I love our morning visits best.

Spiritual Facial

We go to our place of worship,
and in the quiet, hushed space,
we put on our ceremonious robe
and surrender.

We close our eyes,
and in the stillness,
we are enveloped by
melodies and chants
and the fragrances
of lavender, sandalwood and mint.

Masks applied
are washed away,
drawing out impurities
as we cleanse, exfoliate and extract
the useless and resistant
that's piled up over time.

The process can create
uncomfortable and painful moments,
as we bare and expose ourselves
to a bright-lighted magnifying mirror
that is relentless and unforgiving
in its primary purpose to uncover
our internal blemishes.

But after all the poking and prodding
we love the results,
which reveals our clean, pure, and natural self,
now nourished, balanced, and revitalized,
leaving us feeling renewed,
radiant and glowing,
Illuminating.

Until Now

The first time I remember
feeling joy from writing
was when I made a birthday card
for my Grandpa.

I must have been eight or nine years old.
I drew a picture of a birthday cake on the front
with Crayola crayons
and inside I wrote a simple, singsongy, rhymed poem
telling him how much I loved him
and what he meant to me.

I can recall the pleasure and gratification I felt
of being able to create something and express myself,
and my usually gruff Grandpa,
momentarily softened
by receiving my handmade and heartfelt gift.

You have no idea
how I *crave*
at this very moment
to see that card,
to get a glimpse
of my younger self,
that could possibly reveal
the budding writer
I somehow missed or ignored
as I grew up.

Why did I stop writing
and amputate myself
from the thing I love to do?

Numerous fears
and practicalities
immobilized me...until now.

Self-Portrait

By deliberate strokes of his hand,
pressed hard against the canvas,
guided by the One,
midnight blue paint,
reveals a picture
of who we really are,
that many have forgotten,
now recognizable
through the felt energy
his offering provokes.

He made
the *Intangible*
Tangible
the *Infinite*
Finite.

A self-portrait of our divine essence,
the Universal unseen
that has patiently waited
since its creation
for its formal debut,
for the soul purpose
of helping us remember
what is real and true,
however long that takes.

There is no rush in eternity.

PART 3

———

**The resistance from the Ego...
as the Soul emerges**

Tribute to Diana

She died in the depths of winter
just before an unexpected blizzard arrived.
Mother Nature's grace,
extreme, yet effective,
creating a way to seek shelter and turn within
from the harsh realities outside.

We were barely acquaintances,
but I knew her well, on another level,
because she was me in the ways that matter.
The same age,
with the same disease,
around the same time.

Yet, after the initial discovery years ago
of our body's betrayal,
our paths diverged,
her cells, stubborn and territorial.
Surprisingly, her vitality was no match
for her slashed and poisoned body.
She was too alive in spirit
to breathe her last breath in form so young.

I let out a deep exhale and unconsciously bow my head
in profound reverence for her valor that never wavered,
clawing and fighting her way for another day,
by seizing opportunities in the Land of the Living,
with that sparkling smile I never saw her without.

I instinctually walk upstairs into my daughter's room
and gaze down at her while she sleeps so completely,
feeling the warmth of her space
from the forced heat and her sweet breath.

My biggest fear spontaneously grips me,
lodges in my chest and takes hold,
a direct hit to my heart,
that produces greedy sobs,
not the pretty kind.
Life can be ugly at times.
I'm suddenly...so...tired.

I wilt onto my daughter's bed
stung by the audacity of loving someone
with such raw and untamed boldness,
feeling its strength and fragility simultaneously.
There are no answers to Why,
no meaning on the unfairness of life.
All worldly things are fleeting.

As I turn to leave the room,
I notice the snow has finally stopped falling.
I sense that Mother Nature
will work her magic again tomorrow,
forcing me out of hibernation
by creating a silver-jeweled landscape
that will be hard to resist.
I'll go outside and make tracks in the snow,
knowing that under the blanket of white
there is life laying dormant
waiting for rebirth.

Truth

Cracked wide open,
huge waves of truth,
knock me down,
sprawling me out into unchartered,
yet vaguely familiar waters,
disbelief at what I'm sensing.

Unleashed from the constraints of time,
messages from beyond,
disguised in the ordinary,
coded in people, packages,
paintings, numbers and songs,
and synchronistic coincidences,
that puts me at odds
with all that I have known to be real.

False self!
Why do you taunt me,
isolate and separate me
from the mainstream?
The world is cruel
in its judgment of different.
They don't remember.

Resistance softens into reluctance,
clinging by my fingertips
on to useless, yet accustomed ways.
I never asked for this.
Or did I...
unknowingly?

Lovely Divinity,
wrapped in a coat
protected from the biting winds
of uncertainty.
This is the way,
in form,
since doubt is born from the mind
as it projects out into the future.
and Spirit recognizes
there is only now.

Running on the fumes of faith
is my salvation
to my nonconforming and abiding self.
I greet and enter the flow,
emptying into pure surrender.
Nothing is at it appears.
Grace is everywhere.

Mysteries become certainties.
Feelings become facts.
Omega…
there is no end.
Time,
eternal,
overlapping, melding, blending
past, present, and future.

The currents of time
stream through and out of me.
My present self
as the future self
to my past self.
First, awareness,
then, communication.
Is that even possible?

Cyclical and dynamic,
infinity's pulsating energy and vibrations
causing ripple effects
through alternate potentials
in all dimensions
with purpose and order,
linked and aligned
to the minute detail
to become interchangeable realities.

We are One.

Eternity's cavernous presence
blankets me with
awe,
humility,
strangeness.
To *know* oneself
doesn't instantaneously transform
into *being* oneself.
The inescapable transparency
of living my truth
leaves me feeling
exposed and unprotected.

Now,
quiet strength feeds
my rebellious soul,
a willing participant
poised for giving
in the present,
a timeless present.
Truth wins inevitably.

Unwritten

I was born into a story.
I authored more as a child.
As an adult,
I controlled my story,
rewriting it many times,
yet, I was still unsatisfied.
It was never enough
somehow.
I'm sensing now
that I'm not my story.
Though that feels true
it makes me uncomfortable
because without a story,
who really am I?

What is Real?

Is my mind concocting stories
of what could be
or is my soul
tapping into other dimensions of time?

And are these visions
just various potentials
that can slip out of reach
without my knowing,
or my fate,
inevitable and preordained?

Threads of possibilities...
imagination or intuition?
fantasy or truth?
contrived or divine?
wishful thinking or destiny?

My questions take hold,
surround me,
and assault my peace of mind.
Is this the right path?
Is there a correct way to manifest what I'm sensing?
Am I unintentionally going to screw this up somehow?
Do I charge forward and make it happen?
Or wait for a sign to be shown to me?
Do I even want what's coming?

I don't know.
I admit defeat.

And in my surrender
one simple truth emerges
from the exploration
of these things
that offers me some relief
from this relentless probing.

Faith cannot exist
without trust
in what is
and what will be.
Have faith.
Just trust.
And in some deep place in me,
I do.

Pure

Deep immersion
into the pool
of pure awareness,
subtle, elusive and real,
where potentials are actualized,
possibility becomes certainty
thoughts become reality.
Going beyond the boundaries of time and space
where travel is possible
to a place with no edges and corners
at the center of infinity,
the point of creation.

An identity crisis of the best kind,
the vastness of pure consciousness
silences the False One,
with its nonsensical chatter,
who alerts us to all
that is unsafe in the world
that it created
and opens us to actions
that cause more suffering.
Form cannot penetrate the limitless dimensions.

Pure consciousness expands
the Eternal One within
who perceives the past,
surrenders to the present,
and is ever watchful of the future.
The root cause of spontaneous belly laughs
that come for no other reason
than sensing the joy of it all.

Who is this one
who is forever watching and remembering?
And how do I get her to stay?

Authenticity

The crazy thing is that
the more honest I get
the more deceitful I feel.

I'm suffocating
under the weight of incongruity
between who I am
and how I'm existing,
and the clever distractions
that keep me in hiding
from pockets of my life
aren't working anymore.

I want out and I don't know how.
Wait… that's not true.
I do know.
I just haven't wanted to deal
with the demands truthfulness requires
with no guarantee of what will come.

More Questions than Answers

What *is*
my life purpose?
How can free will and destiny
coexist?
How do I know
if I'm running away
or letting go?
How can I plan
for my future
and be present in the moment?
When do I persevere
in making something happen
versus surrendering to what is?
How can I work
toward my goals
and yet remain detached
from the outcome?
When do I ask others
for help
and when do I turn within?
If Truth is nothingness,
how can anything
have meaning?
Can I be okay
not knowing the answers?

What the Hell Am I Doing?

I'm smothered under
the blanket of responsibility
of making my dreams come true.

In the light,
alone with my thoughts,
I feel invincible.
In the darkness,
alone with my thoughts,
I feel defeated.

Is it worth it,
working so hard,
being totally out of my comfort zone,
without even a glimpse
of the Promised Land?
Does that even exist?

I am so scared,
after all is said and done,
that I'll never...
taste the sweetness of freedom,
feel the gentle embrace of love.
hear the laughter of joy.
sense the stillness of peace.

And yet...

Wide Open

Mind is open,
but Heart is closed,
because it remembers
how it felt
when Mind was closed
and Heart was open.

If there are infinite possibilities,
then our imaginations
are actually alternate realities,
waiting to be expressed,
but only when
Mind *and* Heart
are wide open.

Be today,
come tomorrow,
and the suffering will end.

Unrequited

You are Winter.
I am Spring.

The blizzard
has passed,
but your heart remains frozen
in a time and place
by frigid winds
blowing around
gusts of untruths
that never existed
except in the mountains
of your mind.

All I can do is watch
and wait for you
to pass through
the eye of the storm,
with faith
that new buds
will appear
on the twisted branches
of a deep-rooted tree,
by warm breezes
that melt the ice
and lets you thaw
from the big chill,
for you to fully receive
all the beauty
that life can bring.

You are Winter.
I am Spring.
Somewhere...
Summer awaits.

PART 4

The Resolution...
breaking up with myself

Wordless

As soon as I picked her up from school
I knew something was wrong.
My sweet, loving daughter
who usually greets me with a running hug
was quiet,
forlorn,
eyes downcast.

She waited until we got home
to bare her soul.
She was left out,
excluded
from playing with the group.
It hurts.
I know.
I had a similar day.

"Why do they do that?" she whispers.
I look into her big, beautiful eyes
brimming with tears.
I wish I could tell her
the many reasons,
all of which have nothing to do with her,
but she wouldn't understand.

I wish I could tell her something reassuring,
like it will stop
when she gets older,
but I don't
because that's not true.

Right now, in this moment,
what does she need most from me?

Instinctually, I slide over
to her side of the couch,
scoop her up in my arms
and hug her tightly,
tears streaming down my face now as well.
We hold onto each other for dear life,
for some time,
taking in each other's essence.
Sometimes,
there are just no words.

Belonging

Do you ever feel
so alone
because no one sees
what you see?
Their horizon,
straight and narrow,
while yours is
vertical, circular, and overlapping.
They just don't see
what you see,
at least not yet,
maybe never.
Do you ever just feel
so alone?

A Winter's Journey

The crowds are gone,
boardwalk stands closed.
I'm all alone,
bare and battered
without the usual trappings
and adornments
to attract company.

They have all left me in off-season.
The For Rent signs
in front of most homes,
proof of their abandonment...
rejection....
betrayal.

Exposed to the stark, harsh elements,
the blustery, freezing winds
blow right over me
like I don't exist.
Do I matter if no one wants what I have to offer?

I feel cold, rough and choppy,
And the recent storms
have created further erosion.
What will become of me?

Off in the far distance
I see her walking toward me,
slow and directionless.
She comes closer,
and looks right past me
out into the horizon,
further proof of my lack.

I study her,
natural and unembellished,
bundled up in a modest coat,
her eyes with a faraway look,
her cheeks ruddy,
her lips dry and cracked.

She is a reflection
of my own melancholy and discontent.
She too is alone.

We stand together,
yet apart,
for some time,
until unexpectedly,
she acknowledges me
with an unwavering gaze,
filled with strength and compassion.

She bends down
and puts out her arms,
her hands grazing my presence.
I feel her comforting warmth.
In this moment,
she is revived.
So am I.

An unlikely pairing,
I, a deserted beach,
and, she, a wandering visitor,
healing each other,
on our winter's journey,
with the simplicity and elegance
of our presence.

The seagulls,
witnessing the splendor
of our exchange
fly in synchronized V-formations above.

A meaningful life
is but a tangled string
of surrendered moments like this.
All is not lost.

Prison Walls

I don't know
how to leave
the prison I built
from the war
in my mind.

Palatial cell walls
constructed with pride and fear
lured me in
under the false pretense
that I'd be
happy, comfortable, and safe.

The illusion is exposed.

I want to break free
from the maze
of confusion and shame.
Yet, I still can't leave.
Won't leave.
To go where?
Isn't the next destination I seek
just another self-imposed confinement?

What if life is just this?

Breaking Up with Myself

Dear Ego,
Look, we've had a good run.
In fact, this is the longest
I've been in a relationship with anyone,
but the gig is up.

We've experienced so much together,
the good and the bad,
and, yes, you've always been there for me,
but I've grown and expanded
and you...not so much,
and besides,
we've always wanted different things
out of life anyway.

I know you've repeatedly said
I can't live without you,
but guess what?
I can.
That was made clear
when you've backed off in the past
and given me some space,
but it never lasts.
Instead, you keep disrupting
all the beauty and peace
I'm trying to create in the world.

I've been gentle and compassionate with you,
because that's my true nature,
but let's not confuse niceness with weakness.
I can't do this anymore.
I won't do this anymore.

This current round of fear and remorse you're instigating
to create unnecessary suffering within me is the last straw.
I'm so over your flashy, needy, and controlling ways.
And anyway, I'm into the strong, silent type now.

What I know for certain
is that my life will include
my daughter,
creative expression,
ice cream, chocolate,
and a few pairs of cute shoes.
Everything else is a crapshoot,
except you.
There's no more room for you.

Maybe for you
to finally stop,
I need to speak to you
in the harsh tones
that you speak to me.
So here goes.

Your choices,
are to shut up
and get over yourself
or get your bleepin' crap
out of my place
and get your sorry ass out of here.
Comprende?

Eternally,

Your Soul
XOXO

Grace in the Wildness

It's time to say goodbye to you
gently,
yet deliberately,
closing the door
on our time together
and walking away
without looking back.

Our experiences,
were not all bad,
some very lovely and loving,
but the arrival of unstable air
at critical junctures,
from both of us,
created powerful winds
and dry, still air
that, over time,
became an unintended storm.

Surprising to find wisdom
in the eye of the tornado,
learning what is real and true.
There is grace in the wildness.

Clouds of compassion
and mists of forgiveness
hover overhead,
holding little room for regret,
when the focus is on the present horizon,
anticipating the next weather pattern
without you.

A climate change is underway
from hazy smog
to severely clear skies.
It's time to go,
but where?

Pride blown away
by the winds of change,
patience prevails.
I succumb to the unknown,
trusting that double rainbows
follow rainstorms
when illuminated by bright sunshine.

I can now ask for help,
willingly and beseechingly,
to the only One
who can provide the future forecast.

PART 5

The Reunion...
of the Ego and Soul

Tooth Fairy

You came home from school today
proudly announcing
that you now know
there is no such thing
as the tooth fairy.

Hearing the conviction in your voice,
seeing the confidence in your stance,
I felt something solid and black lodge into my heart,
a result of more than the bittersweet emotions
of witnessing you growing up, and
how quickly time is slipping by.

It was seeing you start to lose your innocence,
the belief in the enchanted,
that's present everywhere,
all the time
if we choose to see.

Remember last week when I asked you to water the plants.
You held the hose up to the sky and made it rain,
and danced with joy between the drops.
We saw rainbows in the water's essence
revealing its colorful aura.
We felt cleansed as the water hit our skin,
the grime of the day washed away.

Afterwards, we looked out into the backyard,
smelling earth's perfume,
the beads of water
crystallizing the grass, trees and flowers,
nature all jeweled and bedazzled.

There is a tooth fairy,
but, no, not in the way you've known her to be.
You're mature enough now to understand
that she's not the tiny creature
that flits into your room at night
and puts a dollar under your pillow.

But she is real.

She exists in you.
She exists in me,
as long as we continue
to live in the mystery
and believe in the magic.
Don't lose, sweet girl, what I'm now rediscovering.

It

I'm tired of...
defining myself by other's standards,
controlling their perceptions of me,
seeking something better than what is,
trying to figure everything out.

I can somewhat appreciate
how much wasted energy
has gone into these endeavors,
yet, my mind can't grasp how to stop
the pain, blame, shame game.

Without the ruse,
then who am I really?
How do I show up?
What do I do instead?

A mist of clarity
obscures the air.
I sense
the Knowing
in the Unknown,
the Seeker
and the Sought,
feeling Light
in the Dark,
of being more than one
in One.

Whomever you are,
however you are,
wherever you are
is the way.

All of it,
is IT.

Worthy

They think I'm unworthy
and I've allowed
the shame and guilt of that
to seep into my Being,
affect my thoughts,
influence my feelings,
and impact my actions
because I believed them
without awareness
of my consent.
But I don't believe
them anymore,
which changes everything
and nothing.
I am whole, complete and enough,
and so are they,
even if they don't know it...
yet.

The Middle Place

Caught between worlds,
changing form
like changing clothes,
garments of the soul.

Time overlaps,
dreaming while awake,
life expanding
and collapsing.
I can feel that.

Anything is possible
yet, nothing is real.
The suffering of
trying to find
the answer
when none exists.

The pendulum swings,
far left
and then
far right,
back and forth,
until it finally rests,
in the middle place.

Where there is nothing to prove,
nobody to defend,
no one right way to be,
except centered
between duality and relativity,
wanting nothing more
than what is.

Turning 50

My world has been caught
in the karma of past lives,
where clarity of the Truth
and my teachings
woke people up,
and scared the ones in power
by threatening their authority
because I asked people to trust their inner knowings
rather than the dogma spewing from the mouths
of the latest representatives of state and church.

My ignorance and naiveté about my impact on others,
especially those sourced by jealously, greed, and power
caused me much harm, over many lives,
physically, mentally, emotionally and spiritually.
This has left me stuck to play out a belief
that made me suppress who I really am,
and make me feel separate
from all that I know to be true.

This belief has caused me to leave
the rich imagination and creativity
of a little girl behind
as I grew up into a practical, independent woman
who unknowingly made life choices
to avoid further personal harm from others.

But it didn't work.
Not only did I still not fit in,
but I became judge, jury, and prisoner,
self-imprisoned by my own thoughts and feelings.

And now, knowing all this,
I'm trying to find forgiveness
in others,
and mostly myself.
Only when we can love
our enemies and inner demons
are we truly free.

Rebellious?
Midlife crisis?
No.

Just trying to live
in the purity of the truth
not needing to prove myself to others,
attempting to right
their false impressions of me.

I'm not the abandoned little girl
on the bottom of the stairs
not being heard and seen
for who I am,
a beacon of light,
reflecting rays of love and hope
that scare many and attract few.

And that's okay,
because this light is the spark
that creates the potential
of my deeper dreams coming true.
Turning 50,
my life has finally begun.

Playing It Safe

I thought I was playing it safe
by...
blending in instead of standing out,
going with what was known and within reach
instead of risking it all on a belief of something better,
being self-deprecating instead of stating the obvious,
shooting for acceptance instead of sharing my greatness,
concealing my flaws instead of asking for help,
being practical instead of idealistic,
feeling alone in a crowd instead of
being intimate with one,
being right instead of forgiving,
blaming others instead of fixing it,
appearing perfect instead of vulnerable,
hiding behind an illusion instead of living in clarity,
denying instead of giving,
giving without fully receiving,
staying instead of leaving,
leaving instead of staying,
buying it for immediate gratification
instead of saving to fund my dreams,
seeking other's approval instead of my own,
waiting for permission instead of going for it,
allowing other's opinions to dictate what I
do instead of trusting my inner voice,
pleasing others instead of pleasing
myself, when it mattered most,
keeping quiet to avoid conflict instead
of speaking my Truth.

And...
after doing all this
it didn't keep me safe anyway
because people still judged,
and things didn't go as planned.

There is no safe place to run to in this world,
which is scary
and liberating,
because it finally allows me the freedom
to just be myself,
which, as it turns out,
is the safest place to be.

Rooting for Her

A few years ago,
I discovered the person
who occupies the life
I'm supposed to be living.
She has been out of my mind completely
until this week,
when I came across a picture of her online
and something stirred within.

She continues to do
what I've only dreamt about.
She has my career and accomplishments.
She's hanging out with my friends and colleagues.
She lives in the community I am drawn to.
She even looks similar to me,
a prettier version.

I acknowledge the opportunity
to feel remorse
because she has what I want,
at least from the outside looking in,
because who knows, really.

But instead, my mind is empty and spacious,
and an irrepressible giggle surfaces
that works itself into a full-on belly laugh,
a natural eruption
springing from the surge
of emotions ignited within.

Joy.
She did it.
Hope.
It's possible.
Trust.
The Universe always supports and provides.
Faith.
My version of living my truth
will continue
in its own way,
in its own time.

The way I see it,
all she did
was to get into her flow
before me,
and unknowingly
touched and inspired a stranger
to keep doing the same.

How to Be

Be passionate, but not emotional.
Be visionary, but not unrealistic.
Be direct, but not confrontational.
Be attractive, but not too pretty.
Be accountable, but not demanding.
Be inspiring, but not impractical.
Be inclusive, but not accepting of *that* one.
Be original, but not stand out.
Be assertive, but not intimidating.
Be confident, but not pushy.
Be great, but not threatening.

And now...
no but's,
just be,
for all.

Self-Expression

Words come,
with no censor,
the inner critic hushed.
I like to write
when I'm not there.

Juices flowing,
creativity unleashed,
no rules to follow,
the perfect word found.
More than words
come into existence,
the exquisiteness of truth
coming off the pages.

Fragments of verse
becoming whole stories,
with different details,
yet similar plots,
relatable to others.
Grace in the ordinary.

Surrender finally,
to share my authentic voice
like my life depends on it,
which I'm discovering,
it does.
Writing didn't cure my cancer,
but it saved my life
with the silencing
of my contagious mind.
Self expression heals.

Simply begin
creating something
from the nothing.

Not Business as Usual

The kindest thing
isn't to give them
what they think
they want,
but to give them
what they really need.
I'm not going
to keep hiding
in the shadows,
cast from the shame
of remaining silent,
now knowing,
that with every word
I choose to speak,
I am the silence,
not the silenced.

PART 6

Realizing *and*...
the love affair of the heart and mind

Awake

I live in a world
in-between.
Awake today
for a tomorrow
I'll never see.
You don't get what you ask for.
You get what you act for.
The personal sacrifices of now
take me away
from the ones
I love the most
to do the work
for the nameless, faceless future.
Aren't we all just a bit ahead of our time?

Crumbling

I have this overwhelming urge to run,
not from,
but to.
Raw and wild emotions,
anticipation and excitement
of coming home
after a long time away
to the people I love
that I can barely contain.
But to whom?
And where?

I keep straining my neck
around this invisible corner to see,
but my eyes are blind,
since the reveal of True Nature
can only be realized through the heart.

I want to cry,
long and hard,
for the innocence lost and now found again,
but I hold myself back
because if I start
I feel like I will never stop.

Be bolder.
Look at things from a different perspective,
to go to another plane of existence,
two reach Love Land,
and see Omega,
a place with no beginning or end.
A place beyond belief.

How about Now?

Hey you,
the one with his head lost in the clouds,
hiding behind his purpose.
It's me.
Over here.
You probably don't recognize me
all covered in mud,
trying to figure everything out
and thinking I know what's best.
It's time to stop resisting the unknown
and surrender to what is.
No more wishing for something different.
No more hating and breaking up with parts of yourself.
No more wanting to be somewhere else.
Controlling the what, when, where, and how
to feel safe isn't the way.
Who we really are
only needs now
to access the universal why,
love, peace, and happiness.
It's right here.
So?

and

We are all created from the One.

The One manifests into All.

Since we're All connected to the One,

all that exists is Divine,

which is *and*.

Everything.

It's easy to see that with the good stuff,

but even things we don't like are *and*.

Yes, even ***that***.

The not-nice things we experience

come when we are perceiving Either/Or,

but even Either/Or is *and*,

because it's all IT.

and is a bridge

that connects

to create endless possibilities.

Me *and* You,

alone *and* tangled in All,

We are *and*.

Loving All of Me

You love me best when I'm a 6,
my true self,
soft, smooth, and rounded,
balanced in the middle
between 1 and 10,
but there are many figures of me
that take various geometric shapes
that are also who I am,
in the here and now.

Like when I'm an upside down, over the top 9,
and a 7,
sharp, pointed, and edgy.
I know I muddy things up
when I act like I'm #1,
and forget 5,
with all its complexities,
going from straight and narrow
to curvy and bold,
without warning.

Yet, even with all these factors,
I'm not an equation to be figured out,
a word problem to be solved,
data to be manipulated,
fractions to be made whole.

To make us 2,
to form a unit of 3,
I need you to love the sum of me,
with each as 4,
equal halves of 8,
infinity,
standing upright,
spirit in form,
to create a love worthy of multiplying.

A Love Worth Waiting For

Truth is love.
Love is truth.
To find truth,
be love
with all
in every.
That is *and*.
Love isn't linear.
Neither is time.
Love transcends time.
Time transcends love.
Time travel is possible,
through the currents of love.
Love of self.
Love of others.
Love of this world.
A love worth waiting for
that's here now.

Shall We Dance?

On the dance floor of life
I sense you in the crowd,
yet out of reach.

I know I can't just waltz in
and change the tempo
from quick and hurried
to slow and soft
because I'm not the DJ
in control of the play list
that's already been set.

And now,
even with years of practice
of my dance moves,
I find myself a wallflower
unsteady with my footing
unlearning all my familiar sequences,
unsure of the coming choreography.

I guess we'd figure that out together,
moving freestyle,
improvising
to where the music takes us.

I'm finally ready to dance.
Shall we?

Passengers

You,
can navigate the skies
by reading the stars.

I,
can get you through rush hour traffic
like it's no one's business.

Regardless on how we get there,
we're both on the same journey
to *and*,
riding shotgun.

Epilogue

She finally remembered
who she truly is
and did from there.

Knowing who you really are,
no one
no thing
can hurt you.
Knowing that
you're free.

Acknowledgements

To Mitch Rosacker, a veteran of self-discovery, thank you for taking the journey to *and* with me.

To my message strategist and writing/publishing consultant, Kathy Sparrow, your knowledge, experience, and intuitiveness took a file on my personal computer with an audience of one and made it take flight into a published book into the hands of many.

To Deb Sandella, the shape of who you are and how you contribute in the form of RIM continues to be a game changer in my life, and for the RIM community, for making me feel like I belong.

To Dax and Neal Strohmeyer, thank you for allowing me the opportunity to bring my true self to work every day by accepting me for who I really am and how I show up so I can serve and contribute to something greater than myself.

To Dr. Ken Adler and Lauren Myler, for your care and support through this continuous cancer journey.

To Jean Marie Rosone, who met me at the lowest point in my life and loved me anyway. Thank you for introducing me to a whole new way of being.

To Michelle Zanoni, whose energy work and friendship heals me inside and out.

To Rosemarie Morisco, for our lunches at Greek City and what came from them.

To Michelle Begina, a fellow dreamer who inspires me to make my imagination come to life.

To Aimee Basa, who always dresses my best self.

To the memory of Gary Zambardino, who encouraged me to bring my passion, energy and enthusiasm to work every day.

To Lisa Hall and Joanne Nardella, my soul sisters, even though the demands of life keep us apart longer than we'd like, you are always in my heart, laughing all the way.

To Cindy Whitmer, Cindy Tomcak, Tresa Leftenant, and Kim French, thank you for being my cheerleaders in life, encouraging me every step of the way.

To Patti Noto, Linda Suplicki, Maria Sieber, Cathie Ressland, John Bator, Cheryl Lee, and Jennifer Pellegrino, it really does take a village. Thanks for being my tribe.

To the unkind and not lovely experiences, people, and events I've encountered in my life, thank you for becoming my greatest teachers in realizing my truth and loving myself.

To Julia, Aidan, Sarah, Michael, Steven, Matthew, Daniel, and Gregory and my extended family, my sweetest memories are with you.

To my sister, Lisa Mayer, and my brother, Martin Kaplan, who knew me when and still want to hang out with me! Lisa, with your big, open heart, and Martin, with your calm and steady way, you've made an impact on me from the beginning. Thank you for your love and friendship.

To my parents, Lois and Stan Kaplan, you are a living example of putting family first. Through your actions, you show what it means to be caring, humble, and supportive. I love you and promise to pay it forward.

Finally, to my daughter Mia Kaplan, the one I wished for, for many years, you are my proof that dreams really do come true. My travel companion on this crazy joyride of life, your presence brings me such completeness.

Photography by Michelle Arpin Begina

About the Author

Michelle Kaplan has worked in corporate America for thirty years as a human resources professional with a focus on Organizational Effectiveness and Leadership Development. Her vision is to transform teams and corporate cultures by allowing individuals to collectively bring their true selves to work every day in the form of their unique talents and strengths. Whether strategizing and implementing organizational initiatives, coaching or training, Michelle is passionate about motivating and empowering people into right action. Her mission is to help those she works with reconnect with their personal power to create the outward changes they seek from within.

Since her breast cancer diagnosis in 2004, Michelle has been "walking the talk" by consciously aligning who she is with what she does. With her alarm set for 4:10 a.m. most days, Michelle practices her unorthodox method of meditation, disguised in her early morning workouts, and poetry writing, with the intention of self-discovery, for a least an hour a day.

Her personal story of adopting her daughter from Guatemala was highlighted in Jack Canfield's book, *Living the Success Principles*. Michelle's personal and professional experiences, combined with her natural intuitiveness, provide a uniquely contemporary and relevant perspective throughout her writings on subjects about who we really are that have been explored for centuries.

Speaking loud, fast, and often, no one's more pleasantly surprised than Michelle that her unvarnished musings are organically chronicled in poetic verse. As a writer of fewer words, her natural writing style matches her personal mantra, "Keep it simple. Keep it real." Truth asks for only that.

For more about Michelle, visit her website:
www.michellekaplanpoet.com